Hawaiian Birds of the Sea

Hawaiian Birds of the Sea
NĀ MANU KAI

Robert J. Shallenberger, Ph.D.

A Latitude 20 Book

UNIVERSITY OF HAWAI'I PRESS
Honolulu, Hawai'i

15 14 13 12 11 10   6 5 4 3 2 1

LIBRARY OF CONGRESS CATALOGING-IN-PUBLICATION DATA

Shallenberger, Robert J.

  Hawaiian birds of the sea : na manu kai / Robert J. Shallenberger.

    p. cm.

  Includes bibliographical references.

  ISBN 978-0-8248-3403-6 (pbk. : alk. paper)

  1. Sea birds—Hawaii 2. Sea birds—Ecology—Hawaii 3. Sea birds—
Conservation—Hawaii. 4. Sea birds—Hawaii—Pictorial works. I. Title.

  QL684.H3S53 2010

  598.17709969—dc22

                    2009024829

University of Hawai'i Press books are printed on
acid-free paper and meet the guidelines for permanence
and durability of the Council on Library Resources.

Designed by Julie Matsuo-Chun

Printed by Everbest Printing Company Limited

DEDICATED TO

David Woodside
WILDLIFE BIOLOGIST

My Mentor, My Friend

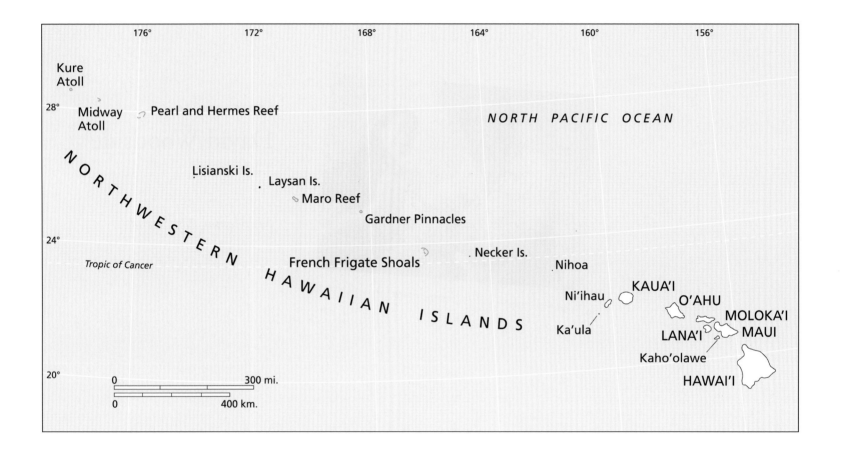

Kure
Atoll

28°   Midway   Pearl and Hermes Reef   *NORTH PACIFIC OCEAN*
        Atoll

                    Lisianski Is.

                        Laysan Is.
                            Maro Reef

                                Gardner Pinnacles

24°
                                                    Necker Is.
    Tropic of Cancer   French Frigate Shoals   Nihoa
                                                        KAUA'I
                                                Ni'ihau   O'AHU
                                                              MOLOKA'I
                                                Ka'ula   LANA'I   MAUI

                                                        Kaho'olawe
20°
    0   300 mi.   HAWAI'I
    0   400 km.

Contents

Preface

Okay, I'll admit that I enjoy watching all kinds of birds. It's my fascination with seabirds, however, that is really over the top. Some folks may think that's strange. After all, seabird colonies are noisy and they stink. They are also awfully messy, particularly if you forget to wear a hat.

My first serious exposure to a large seabird colony was on Mānana (Rabbit) Island, off the southeast corner of Oʻahu, Hawaiʻi. I had come to Hawaiʻi as a graduate student, eager to begin a behavioral study of spinner dolphins. One night and day on Mānana Island changed all that. I found myself surrounded by thousands of terns, caught up in raucous display, fighting over territory, and feeding their downy chicks. Once the sun went down, the terns began to settle down and their screeching calls were replaced with a chorus of moaning shearwaters, visiting their burrows under the cover of darkness. This was amazing! The dolphins would have to wait. Mānana Island would be my home away from home while I was in graduate school.

Since that life-changing experience I have visited seabird colonies in several countries, using my camera to capture images I could share with others not fortunate enough to be able to visit these sites. I have also had the distinct privilege of managing wildlife refuges created to protect Hawaiʻi's seabirds. The highlight of my time as a refuge manager was a three-year assignment at Midway Atoll, near the western end of the 1,500-mile-long Hawaiian Archipelago. For a seabird biologist, Midway is the holy grail.

My hope for this book is to share my fascination with Hawaiʻi's seabirds, both in words and in photographs. If it piques your curiosity enough to visit a seabird colony, then I will have been successful.

OPPOSITE PAGE:
A Sooty Tern colony on Mānana (Rabbit) Island, off Oʻahu.

x   This book would not have been possible without the advice, support, and encouragement of colleagues, friends, and family. In particular, I'd like to acknowledge the great folks who have spent time with me in Hawaiian seabird colonies: Tim Burr, Vern Byrd, Bruce Casler, Sheila Conant, Linda Elliot, Stewart Fefer, Beth Flint, Nancy Hoffman, Jerry Leinecke, J.P. Myers, Maura Naughton, Ken Norris, Doug Pratt, Bob Pyle, Mark Rauzon, Bob and Sue Schulmeister, David Woodside, and Fred Zeillemaker. Thanks also to Jim Denny, Beth Flint, Ian Jones, and John Klavitter for the use of their photographs. Finally, I'd like to thank my wife, Annarie, who put up with the many bird specimens that filled our freezers and willingly shared the Midway adventure with me. I'm still not sure whether there are more goonies on Midway than there are in Washington, D.C.

Introduction

More than 300 species of seabirds range across the world's oceans. In excess of 14 million birds, representing nearly two dozen species, make their home in the Hawaiian Islands. These are *nā manu kai*, the birds of the sea.

While there is no such thing as a "typical" seabird, most species share several characteristics that enable them to survive both at sea where they feed and on land where they nest. Most are monogamous, meaning they mate year after year with the same partner. Most species lay a single egg, and both parents share in the incubation and chick-rearing duties. As a group, seabirds are long-lived; some have been known to live more than 50 years. Seabirds of many species are able to coexist because they divide or partition the resources on which they depend. On land they choose different nesting sites and nest at different seasons. At sea, they may pursue different prey at different locations and at different times of the day or night. Most seabirds have waterproof plumage and special glands to excrete excess salt they consume when capturing prey or drinking seawater. Nesting in colonies provides some protection from predators and helps to synchronize breeding activity.

Hawai'i's seabirds derive their sustenance from the ocean's bounty, but they must return to land to nest and raise their young. These birds use habitat throughout the 1,500-mile-long Hawaiian Archipelago. Before the arrival of the first Polynesian canoes, seabird colonies were more widely distributed on the main Hawaiian Islands than they are today. Harvest by early Hawaiians and depredation by a host of introduced animals impacted the most accessible seabird colonies. Some of the rarest Hawaiian seabirds still nest in rugged cliffs, remote forests, and subalpine habitats. Yet by far the most seabirds in the main Hawaiian Islands are found on the more than 50 rocky islets lying offshore. The largest of these are Mānana (Rabbit) Island, Mokumanu, Molokini, Lehua, and Kaʻula.

As important as these main-island colonies are, more than 90 percent of the seabirds in Hawaiʻi nest in the remote Northwestern Hawaiian Islands on less than 6 square miles of emergent land. The two largest rocky islands, Nihoa and Necker, together provide home for more than 500,000 birds. Midpoint in the archipelago lies French Frigate Shoals, a large coral atoll with a dozen sandy islets and a single rocky pinnacle. Tern Island, at French Frigate Shoals, was converted into a coral airstrip in preparation for war in the Pacific. It now serves as a research station operated by the U.S. Fish and Wildlife Service.

To the west of French Frigate lie two large sandy islands, Laysan and Lisianski. Laysan provides habitat

for more than two million seabirds, including the largest Black-footed Albatross colony in the world. Laysan's hypersaline lagoon is also home to the very rare Laysan Duck. The island's vegetation was almost completely destroyed by rabbits early in the 20th century, ultimately resulting in the extinction of three land bird species found nowhere else in the world. Lisianski Island was also nearly denuded by rabbits, but its vegetation has since recovered.

Pearl and Hermes, Midway, and Kure are coral atolls at the western end of the Hawaiian Archipelago. Seabirds at each site nest on low, sandy islands. At Midway, nesting seabirds have shared the emergent land with a resident human population since 1903, when the Commercial Pacific Cable Company set up shop. In the century since, Midway figured prominently in the military history of the Pacific. At times, more than 5,000 people lived there. The Naval Air Facility closed in 1993 and responsibility for management of the atoll shifted to the U.S. Fish and Wildlife Service. Now, fewer than 200 people share the land base with nearly two million seabirds.

The *manu kai* share the habitat in the Northwestern Hawaiian Islands with some of the rarest forms of life on earth. The Nihoa Millerbird and Nihoa Finch are found only on Nihoa Island. The Laysan Finch and Laysan Duck are found naturally only on Laysan Island. The Laysan Duck has been introduced to Midway Atoll as a hedge against extinction of this rare bird. Hawaiian Green Sea Turtles and Hawaiian Monk Seals can be found throughout the archipelago as well.

ABOVE: *Tern Island, at French Frigate Shoals, was constructed by the Navy in 1942.*

OPPOSITE PAGE: *Seventeen species of seabirds are found on Laysan Island, along with the endemic Laysan Finch and Laysan Duck.*

Conservation agencies are working together to increase seabird populations on Lehua Island by eliminating rats.

Spinner Dolphins are widespread throughout the Hawaiian Archipelago. They regularly feed offshore at night and return to bays and lagoons during the day.

OPPOSITE PAGE: *The Nihoa Millerbird is a secretive, small brown warbler (family Muscicapidae) that feeds on insects in vegetation on the steep slopes of Nihoa Island.*

TOP: *Most of the Green Turtles that inhabit the Hawaiian Archipelago originate from nests on small sandy islets at French Frigate Shoals.*

LEFT: *Laysan Finches were originally found only on Laysan Island. Scientists have moved these birds to other islands as a hedge against extinction.*

OPPOSITE PAGE: *Fewer than 1,200 Hawaiian Monk Seals inhabit the Hawaiian Archipelago. Their population continues to decline despite the conservation efforts of multiple agencies.*

Nihoa, the largest basaltic island in the Northwestern Hawaiian Islands, reaches nearly 900 feet at its highest point.

the Birds

The seabirds that nest in the Hawaiian Islands
represent three large taxonomic orders of birdlife.
The order *Procellariiformes*, or "tube-nosed birds,"
includes the albatrosses, shearwaters, petrels,
and storm-petrels. Boobies, tropicbirds, and
frigatebirds are in the order *Pelecaniformes*. The
third order, *Charadriiformes*, includes the terns
and noddies.

Albatrosses

Of the 24 species of the world's albatrosses, three are found in the Hawaiian Archipelago. Their long, slender wings enable them to glide effortlessly across the windy ocean surface. When the wind stops, however, they find it difficult to land or to take off. Albatrosses in Hawai'i have a prolonged nesting season that begins with the arrival of the adults in the fall months and does not end until their chicks fledge in mid-summer. Once the fledglings leave, they will not return to their nesting island to breed for several years.

Albatrosses at Midway don't seem to care much about the presence of humans. Riding a bike at the peak of the mating season can be hazardous to your health, particularly when birds are flying into their nesting areas. Even aircraft are scheduled to land and take off at night, after most albatrosses have quit flying, to avoid bird strikes. When albatross chicks are ready to leave their nest sites in the summer, it is often necessary to patrol the runway before aircraft land or take off in order to remove the young birds that are getting ready for their own departure.

Laysan Albatross

OPPOSITE PAGE:

Mutual preening plays an important role in the courtship of Laysan Albatross pairs.

The **Laysan Albatross** (*Phoebastria immutabilis*) is the most abundant albatross species in the world and nests almost exclusively in the Hawaiian Archipelago. It is also the second-most abundant seabird, after the Sooty Tern, in Hawai'i. Laysan Albatrosses arrive in their nesting colonies in the early fall. Their elaborate courtship dances and accompanying vocalizations are legendary and as a result they have been given the name "gooney birds." After a period of ritualized court-ship dances, the female of the pair lays a single white egg in late November or early December. During the incubation period, the adult birds will feed at sea fairly close to their colonies. Once their chicks hatch, however, the parents may fly more than 1,000 miles in search of squid and fish to feed their young. By early summer, the Laysan Albatross chicks are ready to depart their nesting colonies. Those that survive the tiger sharks that lie in wait, and the other challenges in the open ocean, will return to their colony of origin 3 to 5 years after fledging.

Numbered aluminum bands are used to monitor the life history of albatrosses and other seabirds. Banding studies have revealed that many pairs return to nest each year at or very near the site they used in the previous year. Living in a seabird colony and watching birds you have come to know can be bittersweet. The parent birds put much time and energy into the care and feeding of their single chick, yet many young do not survive to fledge. There is abundant life in a seabird colony, but death is ever present.

Laysan Albatross pairs incorporate several postures and calls into their mating dance, including the "sky call."

Nests of Laysan Albatrosses are found at Midway on virtually all land not covered by concrete or dense vegetation.

Laysan Albatross chicks are brooded closely for the first few days after hatching, during which time they are fed a rich oil from the parents' stomach that is derived from squid and fish.

With their long, narrow wings, albatrosses are able to fly above the surface of the water for long distances by using a technique called dynamic soaring.

By the time the Laysan Albatross fledgling has lost most of its down, it is ready to leave the nesting island.

Black-footed Albatrosses

The **Black-footed Albatross** (*Phoebastria nigripes*) shares the Hawaiian nesting colonies with its relative, the Laysan Albatross, but it is far less common. The current worldwide population is about 62,000 birds, of which most are found at Laysan Island, Midway, and French Frigate Shoals. Black-foots also have an elaborate mating ritual, but the dance postures and calls are noticeably different from the Laysan's. Occasionally individuals of the two species will interbreed successfully, producing a young bird whose plumage color is intermediate between that of the two parents. Although Black-footed Albatrosses may nest in close proximity to the Laysans, the Black-foots seem to prefer the less-vegetated areas near the beach crest of the sandy islands. They forage widely in the north and eastern Pacific oceans, where they seek fish, fish eggs, squid, and crustaceans. They will also follow fishing boats and ships at sea, scavenging on garbage. Regrettably, this behavior leads to mortality when they are hooked by longline fishing vessels.

Black-foot pairs brood their newly hatched chick for about three weeks, sharing equally in the care of the nestling.

FAR LEFT: *Black-foots are excellent flyers. After the breeding season, most disperse into the North Pacific, with many nearing the west coast of North America.*

LEFT: *Black-footed Albatross chicks are covered with dense down that turns dark brown as they age. They lose most of their down before fledging at about 20 weeks of age.*

OPPOSITE PAGE: *A Black-foot chick will provoke its parent to regurgitate food by nibbling at the parent's bill.*

Black-foot pairs spend a short time together at the nest site when one parent comes to relieve the other as they share incubation duties.

Adult Black-foots may return to their nesting island as early as three years after fledging, but typically they do not nest until they are at least five years old.

Short-tailed Albatross

The **Short-tailed Albatross** (*Phoebastria albatrus*) or "golden gooney" is the rarest albatross species in the Northern Hemisphere and an occasional resident in Hawaiian colonies. Once numbering in the millions, now fewer than 2,000 birds are left in the world. Virtually all of the remaining Short-tails nest on Torishima Island, an active volcano in Japanese waters. A very small number have visited Midway Atoll each year for several decades. Infertile eggs have been laid, but no chicks have successfully fledged. To encourage nesting at Midway, refuge staff have brought Short-tail decoys developed by cooperating researchers in Japan.

The Short-tailed Albatross has been listed as an endangered species. Sometimes the temptation to intervene with such a rare species becomes too great to resist. During my stay on Midway, I watched two Short-tails, a male and female, set up territories only 100 yards apart. For weeks they displayed to any Laysan or Black-footed Albatross that passed by, but they failed to get together. I decided to capture and release the male into the territory of the female and hope for the best. Although they danced together as if this were meant to be, they were back in their respective territories by the next morning and remained there for the remainder of the season. So much for my matchmaking skills. We hope the Short-tails of Midway will nest successfully in the future and, eventually, that a second colony will develop, providing a hedge against extinction for this rare and beautiful bird.

Though Short-tails were once the most abundant North Pacific albatross, their population plummeted to near extinction in the late 19th century when millions were harvested for their feathers.

Decoys made in Japan have been used to attract Short-tailed Albatrosses that may eventually establish a new breeding colony. (Photo © John Klavitter)

This Short-tail dance occurred at Midway after one of the birds was moved close to a second bird of the opposite sex by the author.

Shearwaters

Three species of shearwater nest in the Hawaiian Archipelago. These birds arrive at their colonies after dusk each day and depart in the morning before dawn. Hawaiian shearwaters were far more common in the main Hawaiian Islands before human settlement. Now these populations are limited to offshore islets, isolated shore sites, and remote forested slopes. While these species are typically separated from each other through their choice of different nesting sites, they are often seen feeding at sea in mixed-species flocks. All of the shearwaters are closely watched by fishermen in search of tuna schools. Research supports the notion that shearwaters and other "tube-nosed" petrels and albatrosses can locate food at sea and recognize their nest sites using their sense of smell. Shearwaters capture squid, fish, and crustaceans by diving from the surface or plunging from the air.

Wedge-tailed Shearwater

The **Wedge-tailed Shearwater** (*Puffinus pacificus*) is by far the most abundant shearwater species in the Islands. Their colonies are riddled with nesting burrows, where they find stable temperatures and at least some protection from predators. An individual pair will typically reuse the same burrow year after year. Wedge-tails feed on larval fishes and squid, and they are often seen in mixed flocks with other seabirds, chasing prey that is driven to the ocean surface by tuna and other predatory fish.

For nearly three years, Wedge-tailed Shearwaters were the focus of my graduate study on Mānana Island. I was fascinated by their behavior,

OPPOSITE PAGE:
Adult Wedge-tailed Shearwaters spend considerable time inside or at the mouths of their burrows prior to egg laying.

but they did not give up their secrets easily. By day they were either at sea or confined to their burrows, where observation was virtually impossible. By night, they spent considerable time on the ground surface but were difficult to watch without disturbing their behavior. Marking of known pairs helped me to understand their mating habits, but studies like mine would have been far easier to conduct had night-vision equipment been available at the time.

Wedge-tails are highly vocal. Their ghostly calls are a mixture of cat-like wails, moans, and groans that, once experienced, are never forgotten. On Midway it was great fun to lead island guests on nocturnal field trips into the Wedge-tail nesting areas. Even a crude imitation of their "song" was enough to generate a vocal response from the unseen inhabitants of dozens of nesting burrows.

This shearwater's wedge-shaped tail is clearly visible as the bird flies over the colony.

Vocalization is an important component of the Wedge-tails' court-ship ritual. The bird's throat inflates during its distinct two-part call.

Large numbers of Wedge-tails may gather on the ground at night shortly after their arrival from sea.

It is not uncommon to see Wedge-tails in exagger-ated stretching postures after a night spent inside the cramped nesting burrow.

Wedge-tail chicks hatch with soft gray down. Fledglings will not leave their burrows for good until they are at least 15 weeks old.

Christmas Shearwaters

Christmas Shearwaters (*Puffinus nativitatus*) are far less common in the Hawaiian Archipelago than Wedge-tails. The largest Hawaiian colony is on Laysan Island. The plumage of these birds is uniformly dark brown. Less inclined to burrow, Christmas Shearwaters will nest in sandy depressions under low vegetation and in rock crevices of volcanic islands. This difference in nesting habits may help to explain how they share the available nesting habitat with Wedge-tailed Shearwaters. Christmas Shearwaters are also quite vocal in their colonies and are often heard calling during courtship flights. The single Christmas Shearwater chick hatches after a seven- to eight-week incubation period. It is closely attended by its parents for at least a week and then intermittently until it fledges in the fall.

Early in the breeding season, Christmas Shearwater pairs are often seen in flight together above the nesting area.

It is not unusual to see both adult and juvenile Christmas Shearwaters outside their burrows well after dawn.

*Courtship in Christmas Shearwaters includes frequent vocaliza-
tions. Their calls are distinguishable from those of other shearwater
species because of their nasal, gurgling quality.*

Newell's Shearwater

Newell's Shearwater (*Puffinus auricularis newelli*) is easily distinguished from other species in flight by its contrasting black back feathers and its distinctive white belly and underwings. Remnant colonies are found on the remote, mountainous slopes of Kaua'i, Maui, and Hawai'i islands. Thought to be extinct in the early 1900's, a Newell's Shearwater population was "rediscovered" on Kaua'i in 1947 on a remote, steep slope covered with ferns. Even in such remote sites, these birds are vulnerable to predation by introduced Barn Owls, feral cats, and rats.

Each fall, successful Newell's fledglings make their maiden flight downslope to the ocean. Regrettably, many of these shearwaters are disoriented by the lights associated with coastal development. To mitigate this problem, the electric utility companies on Kaua'i have put shields on more than 3,000 lights. In addition, for the last 30 years, agency biologists and volunteers have been retrieving birds before they are hit by cars or fall victim to predation. They are cared for and released on the coast. The "Save Our Shearwater" project has rescued and released more than 30,000 birds since 1978. Despite this noble effort, radar studies over the last decade indicate that the Kaua'i population is in decline. Newell's Shearwater is listed by the federal government as a threatened species.

The striking black and white plumage of Newell's Shearwaters sets them apart from other Hawaiian shearwaters.

A Newell's Shearwater retrieved by a volunteer is examined for injury before release into coastal waters.

Most Newell's Shearwaters leave their colonies before dawn, but
they are frequently observed seeking food over offshore waters.
(Photo © Jim Denny)

Little is known about the habits of Newell's Shearwaters because of their preference for remote nesting sites. (Photo © Jim Denny)

Petrels

Three species of petrels, all of which belong to the same family as the shearwaters (Procellariidae), occur in the Hawaiian Islands.

Bulwer's Petrel

Bulwer's Petrel (*Bulweria bulwerii*) is distinguished from other petrels in Hawaiian waters by its sooty brown plumage and its wedge-shaped tail. In the Hawaiian Islands, Bulwer's Petrels nest in large numbers only on the volcanic island of Nihoa. They prefer to nest under rocky ledges and in crevices or in the abandoned burrows of other birds. Some may even nest in the holes created by military shells when the islands were used as aerial strafing targets. Bulwer's Petrels are highly vulnerable to predation by rats, owls, and even shore crabs. The population of this species on Midway was extirpated by rats.

The staccato, bark-like calls of the Bulwer's Petrel can be heard at night throughout their nesting areas. An unintended consequence of my choice of campsite on Mānana Island was the opportunity to share a cave with several Bulwer's Petrels. It was in that cave that I discovered the duetting behavior of this interesting species. By observing and recording pairs communicating near their nest sites, I learned that individual birds could, and often did, alternate their barks in rapid sequence.

ABOVE:

Bulwer's Petrel chicks are covered with dark, downy plumage. They will not fledge until they are approximately nine weeks old.

OPPOSITE PAGE:

Occasionally, Bulwer's Petrels will choose to nest in holes left in rocks by artillery shells when the islands were used for military target practice.

ABOVE: *Bulwer's Petrels can climb the walls of the caves and crevices they choose for nest sites.*

LEFT: *When Bulwer's Petrels are observed in flight, their wedge-shaped tails and pale wing bars are visible.*

Bonin Petrel

The **Bonin Petrel** (*Pterodroma hypoleuca*) is the smallest but most abundant of the two "gadfly" petrels that nest in Hawai'i. (The name "gadfly" derives from their erratic, swooping flight.) Bonins prefer to dig their nest burrows in sandy soil. Their colonies may be so riddled with burrows that it is impossible to walk through the nesting area without destroying their burrows. Their digging behavior made it difficult to grow vegetables in Midway gardens— just part of the price one pays for sharing habitat in a seabird colony.

Bonin Petrels feed on fish, squid, and crustaceans, including some species that migrate towards the ocean surface only at night. Colonies erupt with sound when the adult birds return from sea just after dark. Their calls seem almost mechanical. It's likely, but unconfirmed, that Bonins are able to recognize the calls of their mates and chicks, presumably enabling returning parent birds to locate their own burrow among hundreds of others under the cover of darkness. Their nesting season is quite long, extending from August to June. Incubation tasks, lasting nearly 50 days, are shared by both parents.

Fossil records reveal that this species was once found throughout the archipelago, but it is now confined to the Northwestern Hawaiian Islands. These small, largely defenseless, burrow-nesting birds have been decimated in some colonies by introduced predators. Once estimated to number more than 500,000 birds at Midway, a colony was reduced by more than 90 percent after rats were introduced during World War II. The good news is that the Midway colony has rebounded dramatically since rats were finally eradicated in 2000. The Midway population of Bonin Petrels is closely monitored by refuge biologists and volunteers. Birds are caught in mist nets during the evening flight into the colony area and are measured, checked for breeding status, and banded before release.

Adult Bonin Petrels prefer to dig their burrows in the soft, sandy areas of the Northwestern Hawaiian Islands.

Bonin Petrels share their nesting areas with Laysan Albatrosses and other surface-nesting birds.

Bonin Petrel chicks may quickly overheat in the hot sun, so they rarely leave the stable climate of their burrows.

Hawaiian Petrel

The **Hawaiian Petrel** (*Pterodroma phaeopygia*) is a larger cousin of the Bonin but is similar in plumage color. Fossil records confirm that this petrel was once widely distributed in the main Hawaiian Islands. In early Hawaiian culture, the Hawaiian Petrel was considered a great delicacy. According to legend it was reserved for the chiefs, or *ali'i*. Official petrel catchers used nets to catch these birds in their nesting areas or removed the downy young from their burrows with forked sticks or through a hole above the nest chamber. By the time Captain Cook arrived, the Hawaiian Petrel population had declined precipitously. The birds are now confined to widely scattered, high-elevation nesting sites on Kaua'i, Lāna'i, Moloka'i, Maui, and the Big Island of Hawai'i. These petrels are highly vulnerable to predation by cats, rats, and mongooses, and they are listed as an endangered species by the federal and state governments.

Hawaiian Petrels return to their nesting sites in February or March and typically lay their single egg in May. They often feed in offshore waters, seizing live prey or scavenging from the ocean surface. Squid are the primary component of their diet, but they also take several species of fish and marine crustaceans.

My first encounter with the Hawaiian Petrel was on a nighttime insect-collecting trip to Lāna'i with several of my biologist colleagues. I saw a flash of white in the light of our Coleman lantern and jumped off a steep, fern-covered ledge to grab the unexpected visitor in flight. It occurred to me, while in midair, that this might just be a Barn Owl who would not take kindly to my attentions. Fortunately, it was a Hawaiian Petrel who was quickly photographed and released to fly again.

Hawaiian Petrels fly into their remote nesting colonies under the cover of darkness.

ABOVE: *Hawaiian Petrel chicks that leave their burrows are particularly vulnerable to predation by rats, cats, and mongooses.*

RIGHT: *One of the largest known nesting colonies of Hawaiian Petrels is found on the inner slopes of Haleakalā crater on Maui.*

LEFT: *Hawaiian Petrel bones can be found in lava tubes and caves, often in association with evidence of human occupation.*

BELOW: *Biologists in Hawai'i Volcanoes National Park monitor the nesting success of Hawaiian Petrels in remote colonies.*

Storm-Petrels

Two species of storm-petrels nest in the Hawaiian Archipelago.

Band-rumped Storm-Petrel

The **Band-rumped Storm-Petrel** (*Oceanodroma castro*), also known as Harcourt's Storm-Petrel, is found widely throughout the Pacific and Atlantic oceans, yet in Hawai'i it is quite rare. It is a small, blackish-brown bird that sports a narrow white band across its rump. Small colonies are found on Kaua'i, Hawai'i, and, probably, on Maui, where they nest in burrows on steep, inland slopes. Small numbers also nest in rocky crevices on Lehua Islet. They were probably much more common before Cook's arrival than they are today, as evidenced by the widespread presence of their bones in middens on O'ahu and Moloka'i. Like shearwaters and petrels, Band-rumped Storm-Petrels feed on fish and squid captured at the ocean surface.

THIS PAGE: *Band-rumped Storm-Petrels can be distinguished from other storm-petrels by their plumage patterns.* (Photo © Jim Denny)

OPPOSITE PAGE:

Little is known about the nesting habits of the Band-rumped Storm-Petrel because of its preference for steep, inland slopes.

Tristram's Storm-Petrel

Tristram's Storm-Petrel (*Oceanodroma tristrami*), or the Sooty Storm-Petrel, breeds only in the Northwestern Hawaiian Islands and on small islands off Japan. It is a large, mostly dark storm-petrel. A conspicuous pale wingbar across the upper wing feathers distinguishes this bird from other species. Tristram's prefer nest sites under the cover of vegetation. Like its close relatives, Tristram's Storm-Petrel is highly vulnerable to introduced predators. The population on Midway Atoll disappeared after rats were inadvertently introduced there by the U.S. Navy. Since the rats are now gone, the refuge staff are attempting to lure these birds back to Midway by playing recordings of their calls.

Tristram's Storm-Petrels arrive in their nesting colonies in mid-October and females lay their single egg by February. (Photo © Beth Flint)

Tristram's Storm-Petrels were extirpated at Midway and Kure Atolls by rats, but they are likely to return in substantial numbers now that rats have been eliminated at these sites. (Photo © Ian Jones)

Tropicbirds

Tropicbirds are the aerial acrobats of *nā manu kai*. Two species regularly nest in the Hawaiian Archipelago.

Red-tailed Tropicbird

The **Red-tailed Tropicbird** (*Phaethon rubricauda*) is most commonly seen in the Northwestern Hawaiian Islands. Adult Red-tails are mostly white as adults, with a black stripe through the eyes. The bill is bright red, as are the two prominent elongated tail feathers. The largest nesting population of Red-tailed Tropicbirds in Hawai'i, with more than 5,000 nesting pairs, is at Midway Atoll. Red-tailed Tropicbirds engage in spectacular aerial courtship displays that include circular, reverse loops and rapid dives. It is not unusual to see a half dozen or more birds in flight together. They squawk loudly in the air and on the ground, a behavior that has led to their nickname of "Bosun bird," for the Navy boatswain's whistle.

Red-tailed Tropicbirds feed during the day, generally out of sight of land. They can plunge dive well below the surface, where they capture fish and squid. They nest in shady areas, typically under shrubby vegetation or next to buildings or other structures. Red-tails typically approach their nest sites in hovering flight. The rearward placement of their legs, an adaptation for swimming underwater, makes Red-tails clumsy on the ground. Red-tail chicks hatch with soft down that is soon replaced with the black-and-white-patterned juvenal plumage. Adult birds regurgitate food for their nestlings, pushing their bills deep down the throats of the chicks.

OPPOSITE PAGE:

The aerial antics of Red-tailed Tropicbirds are associated with courtship, but inexperienced juvenile birds may join in as well.

ABOVE: *In aerial display, the Red-tailed Tropicbird can change direction quickly by using its tail feathers as a rudder.*

OPPOSITE PAGE: *Red-tailed Tropicbirds land close to their nest sites with a hovering, slow descent.*

Red-tailed Tropicbird chicks are well developed at hatching and aggressively defend their nest sites with loud vocalizations.

Adult Red-tailed Tropicbirds attend their chick almost continuously for the first two to three weeks after hatching.

ABOVE: *Red-tailed Tropicbirds will share incubation duties for six to seven weeks.*

RIGHT: *Red-tails are ready to fledge at eight to nine weeks of age, by which time their down has been replaced with a distinctive new plumage.*

White-tailed Tropicbird

The **White-tailed Tropicbird** (*Phaethon lepturus*) is found on many tropical and subtropical islands. In Hawai'i it is most commonly found on the steep rocky cliffs and forested valleys of the main Hawaiian Islands. Frequently observed in the vicinity of Kīlauea caldera at Hawai'i Volcanoes National Park on the island of Hawai'i and in Waimea Canyon on Kaua'i, White-tails are strikingly white with a black bar across the wings. Two white, elongated central tail feathers easily distinguish this bird from Red-tailed Tropicbirds and terns. Its flight is graceful and aerobatic, particularly when paired birds are engaged in aerial courtship displays.

White-tailed Tropicbirds feed on small, surface-dwelling open-ocean fish and squid. They are most often seen feeding alone rather than in mixed-species flocks. They may capture relatively large fish, in some cases exceeding 15 percent of their body weight. White-tailed Tropicbirds nest in isolation instead of colonies. The varied nest sites may include closed-canopy forest, cliff ledges, tree hollows, and caves.

THIS PAGE: *Because of their remote and solitary nesting habitats, White-tailed Tropicbirds have been difficult to study.*

OPPOSITE PAGE: *The White-tailed Tropicbird is a powerful flyer, able to remain in the air for long periods without landing to rest.*

Boobies

Of the seven booby species worldwide, three nest in colonies within the Hawaiian Archipelago. They share some traits that set them apart from most other seabirds. All lack a featherless brood patch on their abdomen, so they incubate their eggs with their belly feathers or their feet. The chicks are naked when they hatch and are dependent on the attention of their parents. Even the adult birds must find ways to control their body temperature in the hot sun. One method is to vibrate the throat in a panting-like action called "gular fluttering."

Red-footed Booby

The most abundant booby in the Hawaiian Archipelago, the **Red-footed Booby** (*Sula sula*), is also the smallest species and the only one that nests almost exclusively in shrubs and trees. In the Hawaiian Islands, most adult Red-footed Boobies are white, with pinkish-red feet and a pale blue bill. Birds of a darker brown color phase are uncommon in the Hawaiian Islands but are typical of many colonies in other parts of the world.

Red-footed Boobies are colonial nesters, often in the company of frigatebirds. They are highly vocal in their colonies during the breeding season, when pairs engage in mating displays. They use vocalizations to defend their territories, to communicate with their mates, and to beg for food. The male Red-footed Booby chooses the nest site, where he displays to attract the female and then brings sticks to her for construction of the nest.

LEFT: *Red-footed Booby chicks are closely brooded for 7 to 10 days after hatching. Parental care continues until they fledge at 13 to 14 weeks of age.*

BOTTOM LEFT: *Red-footed Boobies in flight will often alternate between heavy wing flapping and gliding.*

BOTTOM RIGHT: *Courtship in Red-footed Boobies involves a variety of visual displays and accompanying vocalizations.*

Dark-phase Red-footed Boobies in Hawai'i may coexist with the white-phase boobies and may even interbreed.

Nearly 40 years ago, I helped to transport Red-footed Booby chicks from a coastal colony on O'ahu to Sea Life Park, a local oceanarium. Not long afterwards the boobies began to nest in bushes within the park, luckily in a site where they could be easily observed and studied. In one study, Dr. Causey Whittow and I attempted to learn more about the ability of boobies to regulate their internal body temperature. Nesting birds were fed a temperature-sensitive radio pill. We monitored their temperatures while we sat comfortably at a nearby restaurant overlooking the nesting colony and were successful in documenting how the birds could avoid overheating in the hot sun by varying their posture and feather placement position.

Brown Booby

The **Brown Booby** (*Sula leucogaster*) is common in tropical waters around the world. Adult birds are striking in appearance, with contrasting deep brown plumage above and white below. Males can be distinguished from females by their smaller size, their bluer facial skin and bills, and their voices. Most Brown Boobies will nest on the ground in small, scattered colonies. Unlike most seabirds, Brown Boobies typically lay two eggs. However, the chick that hatches first almost always out-competes its younger sibling and forces the smaller chick from the nest, where it dies of starvation, overheating, or predation.

Brown boobies feed mainly on flying fish, and they are often seen feeding in mixed flocks over large schools of tuna and other predatory fish. Fishermen in the main Hawaiian Islands frequently report seeing Brown Boobies roosting on large, fish-aggregating buoys. Their ability to dive from considerable heights allows them to pursue their prey several feet beneath the sea surface.

Brown Boobies plunge dive to capture flying fish in nearshore and pelagic waters.

Most Brown Booby pairs produce two chicks, but only very rarely do both survive.

ABOVE: *Adult Brown Boobies are highly social during the breeding season, but they are largely solitary at other times.*

LEFT: *Brown Boobies build a substantial stick nest on the ground.*

OPPOSITE PAGE: *The Brown Booby chick at hatching is featherless and barely strong enough to hold up its head. Within three to four weeks it is covered with thick down.*

Masked or Blue-faced Booby

The **Masked** or **Blue-faced Booby** (*Sula dactylatra*) is most common in the Northwestern Hawaiian Islands, but the species also nests in the main islands on Kaʻula and Mokumanu. It is the largest of the boobies. Masked Boobies typically nest in a depression on the ground, where they may place pebbles or other debris. More than half of the Masked Boobies' diet is composed of flying fish, sometimes very large ones. I recall tipping a Masked Booby upside down to collect a food sample, which turned out to be a 16-inch flying fish!

The call of the male Masked Booby sounds like a high-pitched whistle, while the female produces a loud, guttural honk. Although they often nest quite near other birds, they are highly territorial in protecting their nest site. More than half of the nesting pairs lay two eggs, but typically only the first chick to hatch will survive. The growth rate of the surviving chick will depend on the ability of its parents to find adequate food.

Masked Booby behavior is easily studied using colored bands to distinguish individual birds. That being said, I consider them among the most difficult seabird to band. They are very strong and are quick to assault a well-meaning scientist with their razor-sharp serrated bills.

Masked Boobies nest in loose colonies on open ground, often near a cliff edge where they can easily launch into flight.

LEFT: *Masked Booby chicks beg conspicuously for food when one of their parents returns from foraging at sea.*

BELOW: *Vocalization by both members of a Masked Booby pair is a conspicuous part of the courtship ritual.*

Frigatebirds

Great Frigatebirds

Great Frigatebirds (*Fregata minor*) are one of the most frequently observed Hawaiian seabirds as they soar over the coastlines of all the islands. Frigatebirds nest in greatest numbers in the Northwestern Hawaiian Islands. They are capable of sustained, soaring flight with minimal expenditure of energy. The sexes are strikingly different in appearance. Males possess a bright red, inflatable throat sac. The females have a black head and nape, with a distinct white breast. Juvenile birds generally have a white head, throat, and breast, though most go through a phase with rusty feathers on the head and throat. Groups of male frigates take up residence on the tops of shrubby vegetation. Here they engage in elaborate courtship displays. As females fly overhead in search of a suitable mate, males stretch and flutter their wings, inflate their throat sacs, rattle their bills, and burst forth with loud, warbling calls. Once a female selects and lands next to a prospective mate, she begins to build a nest using sticks brought to the site by the fortunate male.

Frigatebirds are well known for their unusual feeding behavior. Although fully capable of snatching their own fish and squid from the ocean surface, frigatebirds also steal food from boobies, tropicbirds, and other seabirds returning to their nesting colonies from their feeding forays. Frigates chase their unsuspecting victims in an aerobatic flight that often ends with the target bird regurgitating its food in mid-air. In an amazing display of aerial maneuverability, the assaulting frigatebird typically catches the regurgitated meal before it even hits the water.

ABOVE:

Once the displaying is over and mates have been selected, Great Frigatebird pairs will settle into the business of building an acceptable nest.

OPPOSITE PAGE:

The male Great Frigatebird engages in a spectacular display, accompanied by persistent vocalization.

62 Frigatebirds typically nest on the tops of shrubby vegetation or, on some islands, on bare ground. Often they nest in mixed-species colonies with Red-footed Boobies above and shearwaters and tropicbirds below the vegetation. In such situations, unattended booby chicks may fall prey to frigatebirds. The chicks of frigatebirds are naked at hatching and are unable to stand upright. Male and female frigates share in incubation and brooding duties. Frigatebird chicks grow very slowly, and parental care continues for several months after fledging.

ABOVE: *The rusty head of juvenile frigatebirds distinguishes them from adult birds.*

RIGHT: *Great Frigatebirds are highly maneuverable in flight and are able to soar above their nesting colony for hours.*

OPPOSITE PAGE: *Great Frigatebird chicks are attended closely for a month after hatching. Both parents feed their chick by regurgitation.*

Terns and Noddies

Six species of terns and noddies, all of which belong to the family Sternidae, nest in the Hawaiian Archipelago.

Sooty Tern

ABOVE: *Sooty Terns are vulnerable to periodic changes in water temperature that affect their food supply.*

OPPOSITE PAGE: *Sooty Terns in flight over the colony must be highly maneuverable to avoid collisions.*

The **Sooty Tern** (*Sterna fuscata*) is by far the most numerous tern in Hawai'i. In fact, it is the world's most abundant tropical seabird, found throughout the low- to mid-latitude oceans. It is a medium-sized tern, black above and white below, with white on its forehead. Its tail is deeply forked. Sooties are known as "wideawake" terns because of the sound of their raucous calls. Yet they are also known for their ability to remain aloft in flight for months at a time. Sooty Terns feed on small pelagic fish and squid, most often in mixed flocks over large schools of tuna. Their feeding habits make them vulnerable to the effects of global climate changes, as evidenced by periodic breeding failures.

Sooties nest in dense colonies, with as many as four nests per square meter, and in numbers exceeding half a million birds. Their breeding cycle begins each year with birds gathering at night in flight over the colony site. Once they have chosen a nest location, they defend the site vigorously, both with elaborate posturing displays and physical aggression if necessary. Individual Sooty Terns return to nest in the same area each year. Both their single egg and their small downy chick are well camouflaged, reducing the risk of predation.

Though these birds were not the focus of my graduate studies on Mānana Island, I did enjoy watching the territorial antics of nesting

Sooties. The noise of a Sooty colony is deafening, particularly when the colony is disturbed by an intruder. As an entertaining diversion, I tried putting an upright mirror in a Sooty colony early in the breeding season. Nothing seems to provoke a territorial response in these birds more than seeing themselves in a mirror.

ABOVE: *Aggressive posturing by Sooty Terns helps to define the territorial boundary between nests.*

TOP LEFT: *Sooty Tern pairs lay a single, camouflaged egg on the ground, usually with a few stones or sticks at the site.*

BOTTOM LEFT: *Sooty Tern chicks are closely brooded by their parents. On particularly hot days the adult birds will provide shade for their chick.*

Sooty Terns are easily disturbed by human activity in or near their nesting colony.

Gray-backed Tern

The **Gray-backed Tern** (*Sterna lunata*) is a close cousin to the Sooty, as evidenced in both plumage and behavior. The black upperparts of the Sooty are replaced by light gray in this species. In the Hawaiian Archipelago, Gray-backs nest most commonly in the Northwestern Hawaiian Islands. They, too, seek their prey over tuna schools, where they dip or plunge just below the surface. Their diet consists mostly of fish and squid. Unlike other Hawaiian seabirds, Gray-backs may also feed on insects or skinks that they capture on land. Their vocalizations are higher pitched and easily distinguished from those of the much more abundant Sooty Terns. They nest in loose colonies, where members of each pair "parade" in courtship display. Gray-backs often lay their single, spotted egg on or near low-growing plants. Their down-covered chick is brooded attentively by both parents.

ABOVE: *Gray-backed Terns appear to forage for food close to land during their breeding season.*

BELOW: *Gray-backed Tern juveniles are often seen at sea accompanied by adult birds, presumably their parents.*

OPPOSITE PAGE: *The gray back, wings, and tail feathers of the Gray-backed Tern distinguish this species from the closely related Sooty Tern.*

White or Fairy Tern

The **White** or **Fairy Tern** (*Gygis alba*) is among the most attractive and photogenic of Hawai'i's seabirds. It is a medium-sized, virtually all-white bird, with a black eye and a blue and black beak. Widely distributed across the tropics, White Terns nest on all of the Northwestern Hawaiian Islands and, oddly enough, also within the city limits of urban Honolulu. White Terns are most often observed at sea feeding in mixed flocks with Sooty Terns, noddies, and Wedge-tailed Shearwaters. White Terns feed both in daylight and at night. Unlike most other seabirds in Hawai'i, which regurgitate food to feed their chicks, White Terns do not swallow their prey but carry the fish and squid crosswise in their beaks. White Terns hover in flight, making them a treat to photograph in aerial display.

White Terns choose the most precarious of nest sites, often laying their single egg on a tree branch without any nest material at all. The fortunate pairs find a small depression in which to lay their egg. At Midway, White Terns nest on windowsills, fence posts, fire hydrants, and road signs. Pity the fellow who leaves his bike in one place too long, only to find a tern egg on his bicycle seat.

Incubation in White Terns lasts about five weeks. As a likely adaptation to their parents' choice of such insecure nest sites, White Tern chicks emerge from their eggs fully able to grasp branches with their long claws. They wait on these branches for their parents to return with food to nourish them. These birds do not breed until they reach the age of five years or more.

White Terns are particularly vulnerable to major storms, which cause young chicks to fall from their branches. During my work at Midway, my wife and I rescued numerous White Tern and Black Noddy chicks that fell from their nesting trees. We placed them like Christmas-tree ornaments in a plumeria tree near our home, feeding them daily on small fish caught with a throw net at a nearby beach. Most fledged successfully, but some decided it was easier to wait for food to be delivered than to capture it themselves.

It is difficult to imagine how a White Tern is able to capture and hold its prey in its beak and return to its hungry chick without dropping the food.

Fish caught by adult White Terns are passed directly to their chick, unlike most seabirds that regurgitate to feed their young.

White Terns are closely attended by one or both parents for about 7 weeks after hatching.

OPPOSITE PAGE, FAR LEFT: *White Terns do not build a nest, so careful selection of the site on which to lay is essential to help prevent the egg from rolling off the branch.*

OPPOSITE PAGE, LEFT: *White Tern chicks may vary dramatically in color.*

THIS PAGE: *White Tern chicks often seek shelter and warmth under the feathers of their parents.*

Brown Noddy

The most common noddy in the Northwestern Hawaiian Islands, the **Brown Noddy** (*Anous minutus*), is also found on several of the islets offshore of the main Hawaiian Islands. It is a medium-sized, dark brown bird with a whitish gray forehead and crown. Although most Brown Noddies choose nest sites on open ground or cliff ledges, a small number nest in trees on elaborate twig nests. Brown Noddies feed on fish and squid taken from the sea surface or just below. As with other noddies and terns, they are often observed feeding over schools of jacks, tuna, and dolphin fish.

Brown Noddy vocalizations include various harsh, low-frequency calls. Prospective mates and mated birds engage in displays that include gaping to show off their orange mouth parts, head flicking, and the nodding behavior for which they're named. Male birds will also engage in courtship feeding during which females beg for food. Brown Noddy eggs are laid during nearly all months of the year but are most common in spring and summer months. Chicks are upright and active soon after hatching. Their downy feathers range from light grey to nearly black.

ABOVE: *The pair formation process in Brown Noddies involves active calling, flight display, mutual preening, and simultaneous head nodding.*

OPPOSITE PAGE: *The loud, raucous call of the Brown Noddy can be heard from a long distance. Noddies call both in the air and when perched on vegetation.*

OPPOSITE PAGE: *Noddies often gather in large numbers and assume an unusual "sunbathing" posture with one wing spread.*

THIS PAGE: *Brown Noddy chicks range in color from black to very light gray.*

Black Noddy

The **Black Noddy** (*Anous stolidus*) is smaller and blacker than the Brown Noddy. The color of the Black Noddy's legs and feet varies among different populations. Their feet are typically brown in the Northwestern Hawaiian Island population and orange in the coastal colonies within the main Hawaiian Islands. While most other seabirds in Hawai'i are virtually absent outside their breeding seaons, most populations of Black Noddies are resident throughout the year in and around their nesting colonies. Typically feeding closer to shore than most other seabird species, they capture small fish, squid, and crustaceans. They will, however, also seek food offshore, often in mixed-species flocks.

Black Noddies build substantial nests of twigs and leaves in the branches of shrubby plants and trees, but they may also nest on the cliff ledges of rocky islands. It is not uncommon to see both Black and Brown Noddies selecting exposed sites at which to gather, where they engage in unusual posturing. Scientists suggest that they choose these sites and assume these postures to control ectoparasites such as mites by absorbing solar heat.

ABOVE: *Black Noddies display with loud, raucous calls, showing off their bright orange mouth and tongue.*

OPPOSITE PAGE: *Although Brown Noddies often nest on bare, rocky ground, they will also nest in low vegetation or trees.*

ABOVE: *Black Noddies will often roost and nest in loose groups within low shrubby plants, such as this beach heliotrope.*

OPPOSITE PAGE: *At Midway Atoll, Black Noddies may build elaborate nests within introduced ironwood tress*

Blue-gray Noddy or Necker Island Noddy

The smallest and by far the least common noddy in the Hawaiian Archipelago is the **Blue-gray Noddy** or **Necker Island Noddy** (*Procelsterna cerulea*). In the archipelago, this species nests only on Nihoa, Necker (Mokumana-mana), and the rocky pinnacle at French Frigate Shoals. Most Blue-gray Noddies have bluish gray plumage with dark feet and bills. They lay a single, relatively large egg in a hole or niche under a rocky ledge, with minimal nest material.

THIS PAGE: *Blue-gray Noddies will often hover above the ocean surface, dipping into the water to catch small fish, squid, and crustaceans.*

OPPOSITE PAGE: *Relatively little is known about the biology of the Blue-gray Noddy, the world's smallest tern.*

The Cultural Connection

ABOVE: *Bones of more than 30 bird species, including several now extinct, have been found at The Nature Conservancy's Mo'omomi Preserve on Moloka'i.*

OPPOSITE PAGE: *An albatross returns to its nesting island after a long journey in search of food.*

Early Polynesian voyagers who colonized the Hawaiian Archipelago undoubtedly were familiar with many of the seabird species that range widely in the Pacific Ocean. Perhaps some of these species, like the Red-footed Boobies that forage close to their nesting colonies, provided navigational cues to these sailors.

The bones of some seabirds, such as the Hawaiian Petrel, are common in the pre-contact middens of the early Polynesian colonists. These bones indicate that the seabirds that now nest only on offshore islets or in the Northwestern Hawaiian Islands were once abundant along the coasts of the main Hawaiian Islands. Polynesians regularly visited at least two of the Northwestern Hawaiian Islands, Nihoa and Necker, perhaps for extended periods. Surely their survival on these islands was, in part, dependent on readily available sources of animal protein.

The connection between early Hawaiian culture and *nā manu kai* can also be seen in the use of feathers in ceremonial garments and implements. Feathers of boobies, tropicbirds, and frigatebirds were collected and incorporated into *kahili* and other ceremonial implements. Early Hawaiians demonstrated their knowledge of Hawaiian seabirds by the unique names they gave each species. Some names reflect the conspicuous calls of nocturnal birds, such as the Wedge-tailed Shearwater *('ua'u kani)*, Hawaiian Petrel *('ua'u)* or Bulwer's Petrel *('ou)*. The differences between similar species were also noted, such as the Red-tailed Tropicbird *(koa'e 'ula)* and White-tailed Tropicbird *(koa'e kea)*. The Gray-backed Tern was given the name of its prey *(pakalakala)*, while the Great Frigatebird, known for its habit of stealing food from other birds, was called *'iwa*, or "thief."

OPPOSITE PAGE: *The calls of the Wedge-tailed Shearwater, heard most often at night in their nesting colonies, are reflected in their Hawaiian name, ʻuaʻu kane.*

ABOVE: *The practice of stealing prey from other seabirds led early Hawaiians to name the Great Frigatebird ʻiwa, meaning thief.*

Conservation Challenges

Seabirds of the Hawaiian Archipelago face enormous conservation challenges, both at sea and in their nesting colonies. Some species fly hundreds or even thousands of miles in search of elusive prey, so it is not surprising that large numbers of birds succumb to starvation each year. This challenge is exacerbated by climatic events such as El Niño. Warming of the sea surface may make food largely unavailable, resulting in virtually total nesting failure within seabird colonies. Natural predators, such as frigatebirds and herons, also take their toll in some colonies. Many albatross fledglings are devoured by sharks and other marine predators each year. Countless eggs and small chicks also die of exposure during heavy rains or windstorms.

Regrettably, human-induced mortality in seabird colonies constitutes an even greater survival threat than natural causes. The harvest of eggs and young birds from accessible seabird colonies by early Hawaiians was likely sufficient to limit the distribution of nesting birds. At least one species, the Gracile Petrel (*Pterodroma jugabilis*), disappeared before European contact. Commercial exploitation in the late 1800's targeted monk seals, whales, turtles, sharks, and seabirds. Rabbits introduced to Laysan Island as a food source rapidly denuded the island's vegetation. Introduced predators such as rats, mongooses, and feral cats still take a heavy toll on seabird colonies and now threaten the Hawaiian Petrel and Newell's Shearwater with extinction.

Commercial exploitation in the Northwestern Hawaiian Islands did not escape attention in Washington. A 1903 executive order put Midway under control of the U.S. Navy, in part to stop the poaching of seabird eggs and adults. President Theodore Roosevelt extended that protection to the other Northwestern Hawaiian Islands with a 1909 executive order that established the Hawaiian Islands Reservation, later to become the Hawaiian Islands National Wildlife Refuge. A more recent increase in concern about the impact of commercial fishing in the Northwestern Hawaiian Islands has led to additional protective measures, including designation of the Northwestern Hawaiian Islands Coral Reef Ecosystem Reserve in 2000, the closure of all state waters in the Northwestern Hawaiian Islands to fishing in 2005, and the designation of the Papahānaumokuākea Marine National Monument in 2006. In January 2009, President George W. Bush established three additional national monuments in the central Pacific, American Samoa, and the Northern Mariana Islands. Collectively, these four monuments represent the largest fully protected area in the world, totaling nearly 335,000 square miles—larger than the states of Texas and Florida combined.

Although critically important, protective status and new regulations will not in themselves resolve the remaining conservation challenges facing Hawaiian seabirds. Northwestern Hawaiian Island colonies remain threatened by vessel groundings that could result in major oil and chemical spills and in the introduction of invasive weeds and predators. Drifting nets and other marine debris are significant entanglement hazards. Mortality in albatross colonies due to the ingestion of plastics and other floating debris continues. Adult mortality in albatrosses attributable to longline fishing gear occurs throughout much of the Pacific Ocean, far from the protection of the colonies. Moreover, seabirds nesting on low, sandy islands are extremely vulnerable to rising sea levels resulting from climate change.

Scientific research is an important tool that we draw upon to help protect and manage seabird populations. In the last two decades, advances in science have shed much new light on seabird conservation. These include analytical tools for understanding the chemistry of seabird diets and for tracking the sources of plastic debris; satellite tracking for monitoring feeding patterns of albatrosses; ornithological radar, night vision, and thermal imaging equipment for monitoring nocturnal birds; and mitochondrial DNA studies for assessing population structure and distribution patterns.

Kids who participate in seabird management activities learn how to conserve our natural resources.

Scientists can estimate the size of the Bonin Petrel population by banding birds and then recording how frequently they are captured on subsequent nights.

Inadvertent hooking of albatrosses on commercial fishing gear is a source of mortality that has been reduced by changing fishing methods.

Many young albatrosses die each year after being fed plastic debris by adult birds that ingest it at sea.

More than 2,000 tons of kaolin clay had to be dumped from the Anangel Liberty, grounded at French Frigate Shoals in 1982, to free the vessel.

Noxious weeds, accidentally introduced to Midway and other Northwestern Hawaiian Islands, can interfere with seabird nesting.

Protection of nesting and feeding habitat is critical to the long-term conservation of Hawaiian seabirds.

Observing Hawai'i's Seabirds

With some planning, good timing, and a bit of luck, it is possible to observe several of Hawai'i's seabird species on the main Hawaiian Islands. Several field guides listed in the References section of this book provide directions to the best observation sites. While it's possible to see a number of seabird species along most windward coastlines, it pays to seek out those well-known sites for the best results. My favorite site in the main Hawaiian Islands is the Kīlauea Point National Wildlife Refuge. At this spectacular location on the north shore of Kaua'i you can expect to see Laysan Albatrosses, Red-footed Boobies, Great Frigatebirds, Wedge-tailed Shearwaters, and both White and Red-tailed Tropicbirds. At Ka'ena Point Natural Area Reserve on O'ahu you can see Wedge-tailed Shearwaters, Laysan Albatrosses, and, on a good day, both Black and Brown Noddies. A patient observer during the spring and summer months will see Red-tailed Tropicbirds, Great Frigatebirds, Brown Noddies, and Sooty Terns at Makapu'u Point on O'ahu. An early morning visit to Haleakalā National Park on Maui may provide a glimpse of the rare Hawaiian Petrel, and a trip to Hawai'i Volcanoes National Park on Hawai'i Island will most likely provide an opportunity to see White-tailed Tropicbirds soaring around the crater rim at Kīlauea caldera. Several seabird species may also be observed during pelagic fishing and diving trips, such as to Molokini Islet near Maui.

For the serious seabird enthusiast, a trip to Midway Atoll National Wildlife Refuge is the best option. At least 20 of the resident Hawaiian seabird species have been observed at Midway, including the very rare Short-tailed Albatross. Yet, for most visitors, it is the sheer number of birds that makes a visit to this refuge unforgettable. Midway was

OPPOSITE PAGE:

Kīlauea Point National Wildlife Refuge is a great place to see a wide variety of seabirds, as well as Humpback Whales and Hawaiian Monk Seals.

open to visitors between 1997 and 2002 and has recently reopened its doors. Part of the recently established Papahānaumokuākea Marine National Monument, Midway Atoll National Wildlife Refuge is one of the world's most spectacular tropical seabird colonies. For information on arranging a visit, go to the U.S. Fish and Wildlife Service's website for the refuge, http://www.fws.gov/midway/visit.html.

If you are lucky enough to visit Midway Atoll or any of the other large seabird colonies in the Hawaiian Archipelago, be sure to follow "Rob's Rules for Colony Visitors":

- Rule One: Avoid frightening birds from their nests, as eggs and small chicks quickly overheat in the sun.
- Rule Two: Watch your step. Better yet, stay on the periphery of the colony.
- Rule Three: Wear a hat.
- Rule Four: Don't look up.
- Rule Five: If you ignore Rule Four, keep your mouth closed.

Rule Two is particularly important, as it is easy to cave in burrows and step on eggs and chicks. If you happen to step on an egg that has been abandoned for some time, the penalty will be a residue of foul-smelling liquid all over your shoes.

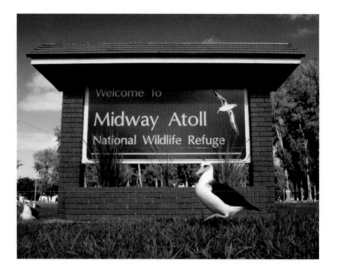

OPPOSITE PAGE: *Sand Island is the largest of three islands at Midway Atoll, lying at the southern edge of a circular coral atoll approximately five miles in diameter.*

ABOVE: *Midway has been a National Wildlife Refuge since 1988.*

Photographic Tips

Seabirds present unique opportunities and challenges to the wildlife photographer. Most species are quite tame in their nesting colonies, particularly at locations like Midway where they have habituated to the presence of humans. Here are ten tips to help you get the best possible photographs.

ABOVE: *Blending birds and inanimate objects can yield striking photos.*

OPPOSITE PAGE:
Capture behavior that will help to tell the bird's story.

(1) Timing is everything. Plan your visits around the seasonal cycle of the birds you wish to photograph. Knowing the daily movements and behavioral patterns of seabirds will also help you be in the right place at the right time.

(2) Focus on behavior. It's relatively easy to capture well-lit "portraits" of most species, but it is more fun and rewarding to capture the behaviors that set the species apart. The observant photographer will learn to recognize when birds are about to display, feed their young, or take flight.

(3) Look to the sky. Some of the most striking photos are of birds in flight, but it's difficult to get shots that are both sharply focused and strikingly lit. Look for locations where the light is optimal and the birds' flight patterns are predictable.

(4) Change your perspective. Get down on the ground to capture a bird's-eye view. Try using different lenses to change the relationship between the subject and its environment.

(5) The eyes have it. The most appealing photographs are those where the bird's eye is in sharp focus. Reflected sunlight or flash in the eye of the bird also adds life and interest to your photos.

(6) Light is all important. Experiment with the direction and color of the light. Don't let anyone tell you that you must shoot with the sun behind you. Try taking photographs early or late in the day when the angle of the sun is more oblique and the light is warmer. Always try to bracket your exposures.

(7) Put your strobe to work. Learn to use artificial light to fill in the shadows when appropriate and to capture the behavior of birds that are most active at night.

(8) Motion is okay. For those behaviors that involve rapid movement, like the bill clap of albatrosses, use a higher shutter speed to stop the action. On the other hand, the blurred wing tips of landing birds result in an interesting and dynamic photograph.

(9) Convey emotion. Your photos will be more appealing if you can capture the relationship between birds. Be ready to photograph the interaction between adults and young or the courtship behavior of nesting birds.

(10) Do no harm. Avoid disturbing nesting birds. Use your longer lenses or zoom lens and blinds to record natural behavior and stunning close-ups without impacting the birds.

LEFT: *Let the golden hour around sunset provide special lighting.*

OPPOSITE PAGE: *Take advantage of all types of weather to improve your photos.*

Experimenting with the sun will often yield special results.

ABOVE: *Seabird colonies provide great opportunities to photograph birds in flight.*

RIGHT: *Fill-in flash can be used at sunset to illuminate dark or shadowed subjects.*

Hawaiian Seabirds

ORDER PROCELLARIIFORMES	COMMON NAME	SCIENTIFIC NAME	HAWAIIAN NAME
Family Diomedeidae (Albatrosses)	Laysan Albatross	*Phoebastria immutabilis*	*moli*
	Black-footed Albatross	*Phoebastria nigripes*	*ka'upu*
	Short-tailed Albatross	*Phoebastria albatrus*	
Family Procellariidae (Shearwaters and Petrels)	Wedge-tailed Shearwater	*Puffinus pacificus*	*'ua'u kani*
	Christmas Shearwater	*Puffinus nativitatus*	
	Newell's Shearwater	*Puffinus auricularis newelli*	*'a'o*
	Bulwer's Petrel	*Bulweria bulwerii*	*'ou*
	Bonin Petrel	*Pterodroma hypoleuca*	
	Hawaiian Petrel	*Pterodroma sandwichensis*	*'u'au*
Family Hydrobatidae (Storm-Petrels)	Tristram's Storm-Petrel	*Oceanodroma tristrami*	
	Band-rumped Storm-Petrel	*Oceanodroma castro*	*'akē'akē*

ORDER PELECANIFORMES	COMMON NAME	SCIENTIFIC NAME	HAWAIIAN NAME
Family Phaethontidae (Tropicbirds)	Red-tailed Tropicbird	*Phaethon rubricauda*	*koaʻe ʻula*
	White-tailed Tropicbird	*Phaethon lepturus*	*koaʻe kea*
Family Sulidae (Boobies)	Red-footed Booby	*Sula sula*	*ʻā*
	Brown Booby	*Sula leucogaster*	*ʻā*
	Masked Booby	*Sula dactylatra*	*ʻā*
Family Fregatidae (Frigatebirds)	Great Frigatebird	*Fregata minor*	*ʻiwa*
ORDER CHARADRIIFORMES	**COMMON NAME**	**SCIENTIFIC NAME**	**HAWAIIAN NAME**
Family Sternidae (Terns and Noddies)	Sooty Tern	*Sterna fuscata*	*ʻewaʻewa*
	Gray-backed Tern	*Sterna lunata*	*pākalakala*
	Brown Noddy	*Anous stolidus*	*noio kōhā*
	Black Noddy	*Anous minutus*	*noio*
	Blue-gray Noddy	*Procelsterna cerulea*	
	White (Fairy) Tern	*Gygis alba*	*manu-o-Kū*

References

For the enthusiast who seeks additional information about the seabirds of Hawai'i, the following publications are recommended.

Clark, Jeanne L. 2006. *Hawaii Wildlife Viewing Guide*. Cambridge, MN: Adventure Publications.

Culliney, John L. 2006. *Islands in a Far Sea: The Fate of Nature in Hawai'i*. Rev. Ed. Honolulu, University of Hawai'i Press.

Denny, Jim. 1999. *The Birds of Kaua'i*. Honolulu: University of Hawai'i Press.

———. In Press. *A Photographic Guide to the Birds of Hawai'i: The Main Islands and Offshore Waters*. Honolulu: University of Hawai'i Press.

Harrison, Craig S. 1990. *Seabirds of Hawaii: Natural History and Conservation*. Ithaca: Cornell University Press.

Hawai'i Audubon Society. 2006. *Hawaii's Birds*. Honolulu: Hawai'i Audubon Society.

Pratt, H. Douglas. 1996. *A Pocket Guide to Hawaii's Birds*. Honolulu: Mutual Publishing.

Pratt, H. Douglas, Phillip L. Bruner, and Delwyn G. Berrett. 1987. *A Field Guide to the Birds of Hawaii and the Tropical Pacific*. Princeton: Princeton University Press.

Rauzon, Mark J. 2001. *Isles of Refuge: Wildlife and History of the Northwestern Hawaiian Islands*. Honolulu: University of Hawai'i Press.

Soehren, Rick. 1996. *The Birdwatcher's Guide to Hawai'i*. Honolulu: University of Hawai'i Press.

Ziegler, Alan. L. 2002. *Hawaiian Natural History, Ecology, and Evolution*. Honolulu: University of Hawai'i Press.

OPPOSITE PAGE:

Be prepared to catch the action.

About the Author

Dr. Robert Shallenberger is a conservation biologist who shares his passion for wildlife through his photography. He received his Ph.D. from UCLA for research on Hawaiian seabirds. During his career with the U.S. Fish and Wildlife Service, Dr. Shallenberger managed national wildlife refuges in Hawai'i and on other Pacific islands, including Johnston, Baker, Howland, Jarvis, Rose Atoll and Palmyra. For seven years he was the chief of the Division of Refuges in Washington, D.C. He currently serves as the Hawai'i Island Conservation Director for The Nature Conservancy of Hawai'i (www.nature.org/hawaii) and vice president of the Hawai'i Wildlife Center (www.hawaiiwildlifecenter.org). His photos have appeared in numerous books and magazines, such as *National Geographic*, *Audubon*, *National Wildlife*, and *Defenders*. To view Dr. Shallenberger's photo library or to download recordings of Hawaiian seabirds, visit www.shallenbergerphoto.com.

Production Notes for

SHALLENBERGER / **HAWAIIAN BIRDS OF THE SEA**

Cover and interior design by Julie Matsuo-Chun

Display type in Avenir; text in Adobe Garamond Pro

Printing and binding by Everbest Printing Company Limited